All These Broken Bones
Poetry and Art by Kindred

For all those who have helped mend my many broken pieces.

Table of Contents

i. The Embers (inspirational)
ii. The Down Trodden (sad or dark stuff)
iii. The Natural (nature)
iv. The Lovers (love stuff)
v. The Misfits (stuff that doesn't fit in)

The Embers

{ All These Broken Bones }

All the broken bones
will heal.
All the telltale scars
will fade away.
What will be left
is the truest, strongest
form of yourself.

{A Quiet Riot}

I will riot,
rebel, revolt, and rage
for the fallen ones -
the broken and the meek;
the blinded and the sick;
the silent and the lost.

I will stand for the ones
who cannot stand
for themselves.

I will rise up,
for I am renegade.
I am rebellion.
And together,
we are revolution.

{ Living Contradictions }

We are all insignificant warriors -
simplistically savage.
We are all miniscule
in the space we occupy,
yet are capable
of far reaching impact.
We are breathing, fighting,
loving, killing contradictions -
each suffering from
a Napoleonic Complex
of our own.
We are all faceless
in the cosmos,
but can be legendary
within our spheres of influence.

{ Fearless }

Instead of coveting
a fearless heart,
strive for bravery
in spite of fear.

Enter the unknown
wide eyed
with your hope and your fury,
your joy and your sorrow,
your fears and your courage.

Enter the darkness
and light it up.

{ House of Matches }

Be dauntless.
Be the riptide
opposing archaic minds.
Dare to quell
the fear-trodden's endless urge
to burden the meek
with bluster and bark.
Be steadfast in your conviction
to sow change
in the fields of injustice.
For fear is a flame
fueled by ignorance.
It is a human condition
that either grows
through destruction
or suffocates into epiphany.
Confront the sickness
and exact the elixir.

Or remain silent,
breathing heavy
in your house of matches.

{Ascend}

Do not give up.
Do not give in.
Never surrender your will.

Strive to ascend.

{Archimedes} (a Daiku)

Be the prototype.
An arc of inspiration.
A new lexicon.

An Archimedes.
An icon of creation.
A true paragon.

{Cinders}

burn me to cinder
and stir the embers
then douse me with fuel
and finish me off
scatter my ashes
to the horizons
of earth and beyond
i will always return
no matter the pain
never to wane

{R.I.P.}

Rest in peace
my scars
my shame
my pain.

No longer will you rip
my threads asunder.

Rest in peace
my fear
my angst
my torment.

No longer will you haunt
my days and dreams.

Rest in peace,
loitering ghosts,
may you taint
my aura no more.

{ Blissful }

Would it not be wonderful
to face adversity,
to face tragedy,
yet somehow maintain
a sense of the wonder
that constantly surrounds us?

{Change}

Embracing change is an essential part
of our evolution as humans.
How can we expect growth
if we fear the method that provides it?

{ Courage }

Be the courage
others seek,
but cannot find.

{Lighthouse}

The world is often dark,
like a blanket of pitch
across the sky.
You can fumble in line
groping at switches
with masses of the lost
or you can be the beacon
and light for them the way.

{Metamorphosis}

If I told you that you could save the lives
of 17 innocent people,
including children,
and all you had to do was give up your AR-15 rifle,
would you do it?
What if all you had to do was keep your guns,
but sign a piece of paper making it harder for people
with real mental health issues to get a gun of their own?
If you had to look into the eyes of those kids
as they were being gunned down,
would you reach out a hand, take that rifle and say,
"No more"?
Or would you continue to do nothing?
Would you continue to clean your own guns
and turn a deaf ear to the cries of innocents lost?
How many have to die before we look into the mirror
and collectively admit that there is a problem?

And that the problem IS mental health.
It IS lax regulations.
It IS weapons of mass killings.

It is INACTION.

What would YOU do to help a broken system?
What WILL you do?

{Daggers}

Thicken your skin.
Steel your hide.
Words will fly
like daggers.
You musn't
let them inside.

{ Shadows and Grace }

I am but a shadow
of the cross
and what strength I have
is but a shadow of Him.

The good in me
is a mere reflection
of His grace and mercy.
They flow freely
through my very bones
and take root in my core.

We are all but shadows -
scant outlines
of the humanity
that we strive to mimic.

Like you, I am a remnant;
a pale replica
of a greater thing -
a living, thriving, sinning
silhouette of unattainable light.

I am an unworthy vessel
only made full
by the act of a sacrifice,
and by a jealous,
but merciful love.

Today I am unworthy,
despite all I have done,
but tomorrow
I will try again.

{Immovable}

Skyscrapers sway
and bridges crumble.
Land masses shift
and mountains explode.
Stars evolve and grow.
Light is pulled into nothing.

Change is possible
when even titans can be moved.

{Greater}

I am greater
than pain,
greater
than loss.

I am greater
than agony
and the shadows
of my grief.
I am greater
than death
and the sum
of disbelief.

For I am the tree
that yet grows
without sun.
I am the grass
that wages war
upon pavement.

I eat my soup
with needles
and make my bed
of spiders.

I toss my fears
to the wind
like ashes
from an urn.
For I am stronger
than the phobias
that once filled me
with concern.

No more do I tremble
under the weight
that burdened Atlas.

For I am sharper
than the sovereignty
of imaginary monsters,
demons, and ghouls,
and the ignorance
passed on
from callous fathers,
friends, and fools.

I am stronger
than the loneliness
that comes with
facing death
and I am wiser
than the lifetimes
that escape freely
with my breath.

For I am deeper
than the silence
that surrounds
the unknown
and greater
than trepidation
from dreams
left unsown.

I am only as great
as the footprints
I leave behind
and only as strong
as the ones
that are not mine.

For our is greater
than my
and we are greater
than I.

{Job}

No matter the storm
or ravenous sea
or rumbling quakes
cast upon me,

no matter the chill
or blustering breeze
or treacherous frostbite
from plummeting freeze,

no matter the aches
or burns upon skin
or grief ridden nights
with urges to sin,

regardless of pain
and my vanishing breath
from the harrowing truth
of an innocent's death,

no matter the space
or distant between
my home is the heavens -
the kingdom unseen.

{Conquer}

I am of the dauntless,
of the steadfast,
the unrelenting.

I am of the faithful,
of the savage,
the intrepid
who strive to rise above
even in the face
of the insurmountable.

I will conquer
or die trying.

{Roses}

We have moved mountains
and pierced the heavens,
but can we not stop
to simply smell the roses?

{ Philosophical Mantras, of Sorts }

Think wisely.
Give freely.
Speak earnestly.
Act justly.
Smile frequently.
Live fully.
Love wildly.

{Once Forgotten}

Hush
This reminds me of something.
This reminds me
of a memory once forgotten;
of a void once filled
with moments of happiness.

Stop
This feels like an ache.
This feels like an ache
from a wound once healed;
from a scar once bleeding
with poisons of sin.

Shout
with all of your voice
and all of your anger;
with all of your reason
and all of your love.

Cry.
Shout.
Speak out
with fists raised
and guns holstered.

Be voiceless no more.

{Pilgrimage}

Are we not but specs
in the vastness,
lacking substance
until viewed in scope?

Are we not simple creatures
looked upon with jealous eyes,
looked upon with reverence?
A deep envy and admiration
often undeserving for such
wicked, prideful,
and thankless beings.

Should we mimic
the humble and quiet trees,
perhaps then we will earn
the selfless sacrifice
and eternal ardor
that was freely given
on a hillside
so long ago.

{ Prayer of the Petrified }

Even if my skin begins to petrify
and my arms branch out wide;
even if my legs turn to roots
and anchor into the depths
for grip and nourishment,
I will continue to pray
and give thanks.

{ Siren }

The allure of perfection
is a dangerous thing.

{Original Copy}

It is a rare feat to be wholly original.
There are very few things
that have not been said,
done, or written.
Just be open and honest,
and always true to yourself.

{Beautiful World}

This is a beautiful world
so long as we allow it to be.
We are the only creatures
with the ability to change that,
for better or worse.

{Masks}

When the world sees a mask,
choose to see the beauty within.

{Concrete}

The smallest blade of grass
can find its way
through the densest
of concrete.

{Conquer}

As long as there is fear
and hatred in our hearts
there is something more worthy
of conquering
than each other.

{Dirt}

No matter how thick
the dirt upon you
it can be washed away.

{Exhale}

Breathe in fear,
exhale courage.

{ Family }

Family is everything –
Truth, love, and happiness.

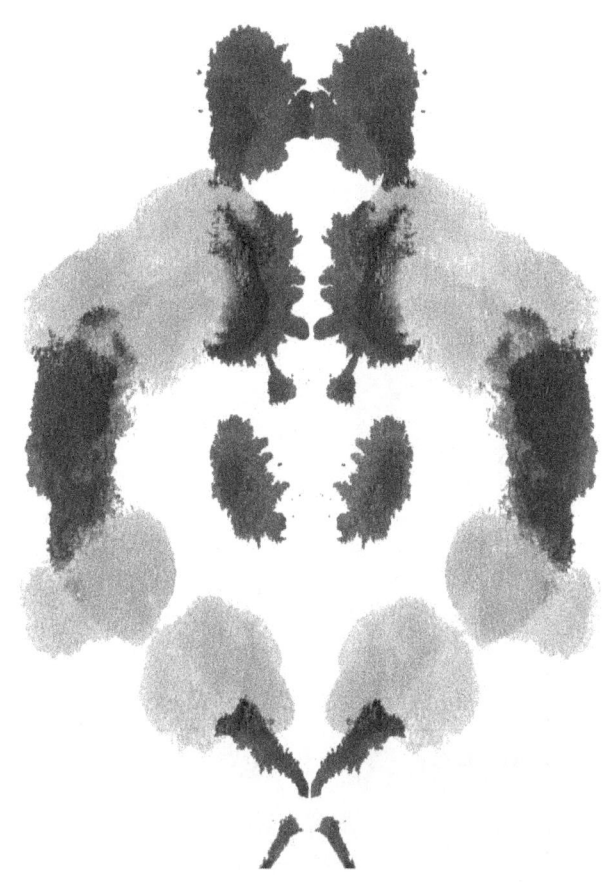

{ Parachute }

We must have dauntless belief
in the courage of our conviction -
like being strapped to a faulty parachute
and jumping anyway kind of faith.

{ Heavy Break }

Life can be heavy,
but I don't have time to shatter.

{Future Blind}

You cannot plan for the future
while blind to the mistakes of the past.

{Growth}

Grow tomorrow
by learning from yesterday.

{Armed}

The greatest weapon
evil has at its disposal
is our collective inaction.

{ Eyes of Hope }

All is within view
through the eyes of hope,
beneath the light of love.

{Who I Am}

I am who I am
not only from my mistakes,
but also in spite of them.
I can only hope to make many more.

{ Mold Breaker }

I don't mind being a mold
for those who walk behind me,
but I prefer
to be a mold breaker.

{ Mountain Top }

We grow more in the valley
than on the mountain top.

{Pathfinder}

Instead of treading the path before you,
leave a new path in your wake.

{Compassion}

Carry peace in your hands
and compassion
in your soul.

{Perfect Illusion}

Perfection is an illusion.
Perseverance is real.

{ Year of the Lion }

Each new sunrise
brings a chance to improve.
Lions don't need resolutions.

{Tidals}

Be more than a mere ripple
amid swollen tides.
Make waves
and let them propel you.

{Seeker}

Seek knowledge,
discover purpose.

{ Quiet Hearts }

A heart knows only
what it is taught –
Deeds undone and silent tongues,
it knows them not.

{ Age of Bones }

Age is not told by our bones,
but only by our souls.

{Soul Storm}

To love without your whole heart
is a storm on the soul.

{Spawn Creation}

Surround yourself with creativity
and you will spawn creation.

{ Stand Idle }

Who are we to have ability,
yet do nothing?
I, for one,
will not stand idle.

{Legacy}

Time will lay you to rest,
but your legacy lives on
through words and deeds.

{Shadow Puppets}

I am well versed in the art
of shadow puppetry.
Lurking inside,
the shadows dance
their rhythmic choreography.
They creep and sway
and they grow and prey.
They twist into the marrow
and the sinewy bits of my being.

Only deep, penetrating light
can quell the desire
to rule over their host.
The kind of light
that seeps from my pores
and bursts from the tips
of my tired fingers.

Within, we are capricious
fusions of shadow and light;
some may darken the day,
others were born to ignite.

{Folly}

Inaction was yesterday's bane,
today's idle folly,
and tomorrow's destruction.

{ Rise }

I am a Goliath
hiding the heart of David.
I am the rock of Gibraltar
presiding over perilous seas.
I am the Lord of lands -
the one and true king.

I am an endless,
ever expanding tapestry
of blood, bone, and will.
I will consume my enemies
like a tsunami on the shore.

I will not give in to fear,
nor hatred,
nor agony.
I will redefine
the meaning of

RISE.

{ Scars }

Why do we keep the scars
that make us,
only to hide the ones
that break us?

Keep those markings
displayed in full view
for they are the language
of a beautiful you.

{The Dark Tree}

Even a dead tree
can grow beneath the gaze of light.

And the crestfallen heart -
it too shall rise with shadows
in the mid-day sun.

For light can pierce
the darkness of oblivion,
and it shines in many forms -
some are witnessed
and some are lit from within.

{Winged}

Precious soul,
you were born to fly
and to quake
the imagination
of this static world.

Why stay grounded
when you were given
such masterful wings?

The Down Trodden

{Knife}

I said I would
take a bullet for you,
not a knife in the back.

{ The Prophecy of Cinder }

When flame seeks fodder
and forges its own path,
light will thus extinguish
and the darkness will rise.

In this time of great reckoning
the only light that shall be
is that born of spark -
that which consumes
ash and bone
and breathes forth *Cinder*.

When light collapses
and night bubbles up
from the fissures
and crevices
like rivers of pitch,
Cinder will thus usurp
the Bearer of Light.

A new epoch will be
thrust into motion -
one in which the boundaries
of the three realms melt away.
Vista - where the winged lights dwell,
Preoath - land of the walkers,
and Underoath - the realm of shadows,
will all merge into one fluid existence -
Oathvex.

Only the strongest of lights
will survive the reckoning.
Only the brightest of souls
will bear witness.

{Sin}

I am the bearer
of black souls,
the ruler of the wretched
and the nameless.
I am the true father
of bastards.
Only the damned
may speak my name.

I am cinder and ash;
the brimstone
and the flame.
I am the searing heat
that cripples your flesh
and scars your soul
with bitterness and shame.

I am the hunger
that eats you
from within.

I am the lurking,
seductive
touch of sin.

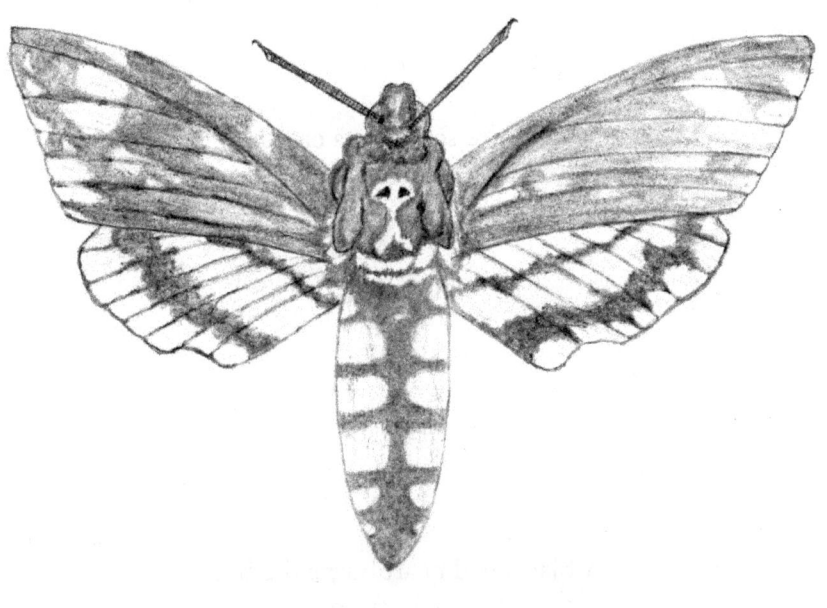

{ Blood and Bones }

It's hard to escape the demons
when they reside within
like blood and bones.

They stalk our trials and triumphs
like shadows of dark deeds
done upon thrones.

We bend a knee to fearsome will
like knights before a king
dulled by ill pride

We're set upon a crucible
of doubtful self loathing,
then cast aside.

It is hard to hide skeletons
when they laugh, and rattle,
and brashly goad.

It is hard to quell the twilight
when it sings seductions
in a wild ode.

A blackened heart burns the hottest,
like an acetylene pyre
with coals of sin.

A spirit wrapped in evil's wings
will be consumed by flames
from deep within.

{Feel Something}

I just want to feel something
that doesn't feel like it's killing me.

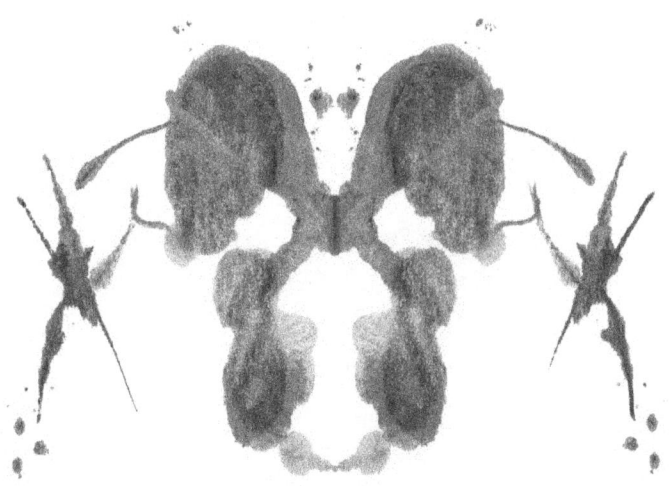

{Asylum}

Provide asylum
to this low, outcast creature -
it covets assent.

{ Silent Cycle }

Alone.

Alone

and silent.
Silently lost.
Lost and found.
Found and loved.
Loved and lost.
Lost and

alone.

Alone.

{ Predator and Prey }

Where there are lions
there are herds
fighting to be spared.

Where there are sharks
there are prey
destined to be snared.

Where there is fear
there is an alpha
fresh upon its scent

and where there is defeat
there are howls
of failure's lament.

The Natural

{Drops}

If your eyes
are always focused
on muddy water
you'll never find
the beauty in the raindrop.

{Endangered}

Is the earth not alive?
Does she not grow,
and cry, and bleed?
The earth, herself,
is an endangered species
and we humans
are the poachers -
draining, chopping,
and burning
until her very essence
has been siphoned
and she lives no more.
Nor shall we.

{Lumberjack}

Outside my window
stands a tree -
majestic and wise in years.

On that tree
lives a squirrel,
with frayed fur
and a twitching nose.

Neighboring the squirrel,
a chipmunk darts
from limb to limb,
cheeks bulging with
the fruits of his labor.

Above them both,
nests a lark -
a lovely songbird
patiently awaiting
her spotlight.

Outside my prison
rises an ax

and I am shackled
by progress.

{Symphonic}

I wake in moonlight dew
and decipher the language
of the stars.
A vast twinkling symphony
of cosmic Morse code
telling me I should be sleeping.

And night owls croon
a mournful sounding ode -
soloist pleas
worthy of an amphitheater.

The locusts, too,
shrill in their advice;
spiked legs like tiny violins
imploring me to rest.

Soon, I'll heed their counsel.
But for now,
I only wish
to enjoy the music.

{ Where Flies the Bluebird }

Where flies the bluebird
when spring showers impede,
when swift fall the raindrops
like a galloping stampede?

Where swims the koi fish
when drought drinks the pond,
when parched become the clouds
and dunes stretch beyond?

Where flows the river
when ice steals its form,
when nature takes its due
within an arctic storm?

Where prays the mantis
when trees shed their limbs?
Where flies the bluebird
when daylight swiftly dims?

{Shades}

For the sun glides in blue
and the moon is engulfed in black.
For our earth is painted with umber
and springs push out the clear.
For our hands gift the red
and our feet trample the green.
For the birds pierce the white
and the bees dance in yellow.
For every shade of every color
exists in the spectrum of being
and every eye should catch sight
of a light that is worth seeing.

For hearts the color of released
and souls a shade of unleashed.

{ Sequoia }

With strength intertwined
like intersecting vines
or roots twisting below
patches of firs and pines

or the conglomerate of power
in a sequoia base
that binds to the earth
and rarely gives chase

to the persuasion of winds
and the shifting of stones
that wreck lesser things
like dry branches and bones,

hold fast to your love
and let go of your sin
to blossom in life
and grow stronger within.

{ March of life }

A robin bending a branch.
Snow churning in the clouds.
The breeze crystallizing breath.
A mountain swallowed by perspective.

The profound march of life
drums ever-onward.

The Lovers

{ Sparks }

Your breath heralds
the approaching dawn
and calms nocturnal beasts.

Your gaze can boil the blood
and haunt the dreams
of slumbering giants.

Your whisper carries
like an echo of tomorrow,
piercing the hollows of the empty.

Your smile stirs
the dying and the fallen,
the living and the risen.

Your spark can awaken
dormant volcanoes
and reignite dying suns.

A torch, vivid in the vast,
you bestow light in a realm
once subdued by darkness.

{ Grovel }

Ego be damned -

I would gladly
grovel at your feet
if it would
bring me closer
to your lips.

{ Sixth Sense }

What do we have
if not hands for touching,
eyes for gazing,
and the power to scent
attractive pulses?

What do we have
if not a voice for whispers,
a lively tongue
for tasteful pleasures,
and an ear to welcome
sweet nothings?

What do we have
if not the sense to love?

{Ageless}

I will always love you
with no hesitation
nor limitation;
beyond boundary,
and in the face
of consequence.

Unfettered.
Unaging.
Unconditional.

{Untwist}

I am loose threads -
pull me into knots.

Tie me up.
Tie me up,

pull me taut,
then untwist me.

{Lover}

Am I not your Eros,
your Adonis,
your Pothos?

Am I not your Romeo,
your Valentino,
your personal Casanova?

Am I not your ceaseless Lancelot,
your Hades defying Odysseus,
your ode penning Orpheus?

Am I not your libertine lover,
ready to appease
at your behest,
my muse?

{Daylight}

She is my light.
When she is not near,
my day grows dim.

When she is gone from me
the whole world goes dark,
baleful, and grim.

She is my daybreak,
my harbinger of sun
in the midst of bad dreams.

She is luminescent,
a torch in the bleak night
whispering with moon beams.

She is my daybreak,
dancing across the veil -
my resounding dawn,
my daylight nightingale.

{Capacity}

I have this love -
I am rich with it.
It overflows the brim
and spills upon the earth
at your feet.

I have all this love,
I know not what to do with it.
So I give it to my world -

so I give it to you.

{Weather}

It's always bad weather
when we're not together.

{ Tides }

Just as all tides
are slave to the moon,
I am bound
to the command
of your glance,
pulled in with the allure
of your gravity.

You are the moon,
its cosmic force,
and the swelling tides.
I am powerless -
helplessly captive
in your wake.

{ Artist }

I strive to make art every day,
if only in the way that I love you.

{ Magnum Opus }

She is my entire journey
and the destination
I have toiled to reach.

She is my pinnacle stroke.
My coveted Nobel prize
and my shining Pulitzer.

She is my literal life's work.
My sole piece of nonfiction.
My greatest achievement.

She is my magnum opus.

{ The Summer }

My breath is heavy
in the air.
My fingers
are frozen crystals.

My chest is an icebox
and my heart beats slow.

I am a glacier -
a drifting iceberg
in a sea of frost.

But you -
you are the summer;
the blistering heat
from a generous sun.

You are the warmth
that thaws me
to my shivering bones.

To melt away
my icy layers
I need only
to bask in you.

{ Atom Smashers }

Here we are,
throwing ourselves
together
like atom smashers,
discovering what new
particles
we can create.

{ Firework }

You quake my chest
and glow my eyes
like blooming flares
across the skies.

You shake my bones
and steal my air
and spark my mind
out of despair.

My beautiful bedlam,
my skyborn caprice.
My riotous prism -
moonlight masterpiece.

{ Wildfire }

Your beauty
is the wind.
Your kiss
is the spark.
And my love -
that is
the wildfire.

{Fathomless}

Just as the sky contains
immeasurable depth
and the spirit can endure
endless sorrows;

just as the sea conceals
a billion forms of life
and the mind conceives
a billion inspired thoughts;

just as an abyss
can be unbounded
and space exhibits
an infinite array of horizons

so too, exists my adoration.
So too, extends my love
far into the maze
of time and existence.

Profound.
Liberated.
Fathomless.

{ Boundless Light }

There is boundless
hope within her
and it glows
perpetually
like the light
of the universe.

{It is}

It is
It is beautiful
It is beautiful love
It is beautiful love
as you grace my morning
with your splendor
It is beautiful love
It is beautiful
It is

{Quiver}

a touch on fire
a pull of desire
bodies brought to shiver
even our bones will quiver

a kiss of skin
ancient discipline
a collision of sweat and flesh
unabated desires mesh.

{ Blind Faith }

In spite of everything,
and in the midst of this scratch and sniff,
try before you buy society,
I still love you -
for all of the things I know,
but especially
for all of the things
I have yet to learn.

{The 3rd Stage of Love}

Hold on to me
with the conviction
of rigor mortis

and don't let go,
even beyond
the certainties of death.

{ Be Still }

You are still my lighthouse,
my anchor,
my harbor.

You are still my waypoint,
my course,
my compass.

You are still my current,
my sail,
my tide -

for whom I still write;
of whom I still dream.

{ Paper Lanterns }

She is a paper lantern
in the night sky,
dancing in the face
of a mourning moon.
Like a warm light,
soft and inviting;
a relentless glow
in the midst of darkness.
She is an extolment of life -
unchained and tenacious,
hurling herself freely
at an unforgiving world.
She is brazenly strong
in the face of small minds
and narrow hearts.
Like paper lanterns,
she cares not of the what-ifs
and the should-have-dones.
She is a symbol
that our dreams
and our memories
travel with us
like lanterns in the breeze.
She carries with her
not sadness or remorse,
but peace -
peace and hope
for the nights to come.

{Modern Wonder}

She is the brightest,
most true wonder of my world.

{Lips}

From the moment
that I kissed you
my lips would not
dare resist you.

{ Gales and Larks }

Love her as much
with the morning larks
as you do
with the nightingales.

{The 8th Day}

On the 8th day
God attempted perfection.
With His breath
He stirred the stardust
and with His very hands
He blended strength, wisdom,
bliss, and beauty -
thus, you were forged.

A stunning creation.
A meticulously crafted sculpture.
A finely-tuned musical instrument
standing out in a glorious symphony.

But alas, shy of perfect.
Even the greatness
of the Allfather
was not enough
to eclipse the threshold
of perfection.

Still, you are a glimpse
of that immaculate endeavor
set forth of the 8th day
of creation.

{Beautiful Allusion}

In a world of white swans
you are a resplendent
black feather.

Cascading in the wind,
teasing subtle glimpses
of a rare masterpiece.

{With You}

I am with you
whenever.
Forever.

{ Resurrection }

destroy me with those eyes
revive me with those lips

{ Mistress Moon }

The moon is my mistress,
my celestial muse -
the most seductive
of heavenly bodies.

Wheresoever
she hovers,
find me there
gazing, loving, pining.

And wheresoever
lands her moonlight,
be it mountain or sea,
find me there
kneeling, hoping, grasping.

I shall slumber eternal
under the shine
of a jealous sun,
awaiting the return
of my mistress moon.

{ Into the Light }

The flashing beacon
of a lighthouse,
the intense glare
of our fiery sun,
the hypnotic flicker
of a billion stars,
the epic burst
of a supernova -
all dim in comparison
to the blaze of your shine.

{ Weakness }

There is weakness in me.
Oh, how I feel it.
It echoes through my chest
and slithers down my spine.

There is weakness in me -
it makes a home in my knees.
They seem to buckle
each time you speak to me.

{On This Day}

On this day
when a mountain bends;
on this day
when poverty ends;
when waves deny the shore,
on this day
I will love you no more.

On this day
when trees melt beneath the sun;
on this day
when a pair is merely one;
when clouds refuse to ascend,
on this day
my love for you will end.

When rocks rise up from the ground
and a siren makes not a sound;
when feats of fiction prove true,
on this day,
I will no longer love you.

{When No One is Watching}

When no one is watching
are you as lovely as you seem?
When every eye is closed
are you still perfection's dream?

Does your beauty exist
when light no longer holds sway?
When no one is watching
will your glory fade away?

Your lips steal my breath
each time they recite my name,
but when no one is there to see,
I'll suffocate just the same.

{Touch, Burn, Repeat}

I live and die in these moments,
in every touch.
I am burned and born again
like a phoenix.
A cyclic dance
of scorching skin.
Like bonfire ashes,
I drift into the abyss
where there is nothing,
save for my desire
to be renewed

again
and again.

{The Dark}

I don't always need you
to push back the night.
Or to be the brilliant glow
that casts out the terrors.

I need you to be the darkness
and wrap me in amaurotic shadow.
Eclipse the true horrors of reality
with your flowing, Cimmerian shade.

I am not afraid of darkness;
I am scared of what I find
when I turn on the lights
and you are not here.

{ She is Music }

She has lyrics in her blood,
rhythm in her bones,
and music in her soul.

{ Heaven }

If I must,
I'll bring Heaven to you,
into all that we are,
throughout all that I do.

{ A Dance of Flames }

Your second skin
loosely scattered.
Your sweet modesty
softly shattered.
Your vulnerable flesh,
like a fresh peach;
its sweetness lingers
as I further my reach.
We become oblivious
to peering eyes.
Tangled up,
echoing sighs.
Surviving on desire,
with unquenchable thirst.
Our friction sparks a fire
in a dance well rehearsed.
Your heat spreads wide
like angel wings
consuming me whole
as our passion sings.

Your breath feeds the flame,
Your fire calls my name.

{ A Star Named Adalore }

I searched the heavens
for the most stunning light
to ever exist.

I found such a star
and named it after you.
In an ancient galaxy,
it still burns bright.

I imagine its nearby stars
feel envious of the honor
of being named after
the most gorgeous object
in the universe.

{ Hope Tomorrow }

It isn't much,
but it may be all I have to give.
It is yours to hold
if you wish
until we no longer need it.
You might call it *tomorrow*,
but I call it *hope*.

{ Into You }

Drop the flame
into my lap
and let it swirl.
Blow the wind
and let it feed.
Combustion swells into
emotion,
into lust -
lustful love.
Let the flames
breathe it in
and spread over my body,
consuming all that is desired.
Savor the taste
like sustenance
washing over hunger.
Sparks rage into passion.
Into lust.
Into love.
Into you.

{Devours Me}

The temptation devours me.
I am consumed.
I am saturated by its warmth.
It loves me, and I, it.
The temptation to touch you.
The need to have you.
The desire to know you,
all of you,
like no other has nor will.
Embers blaze within the fire -
a fire that has scorched
my will to resist.
I am a humble servant to my lust.
The temptation has devoured me.

The Misfits

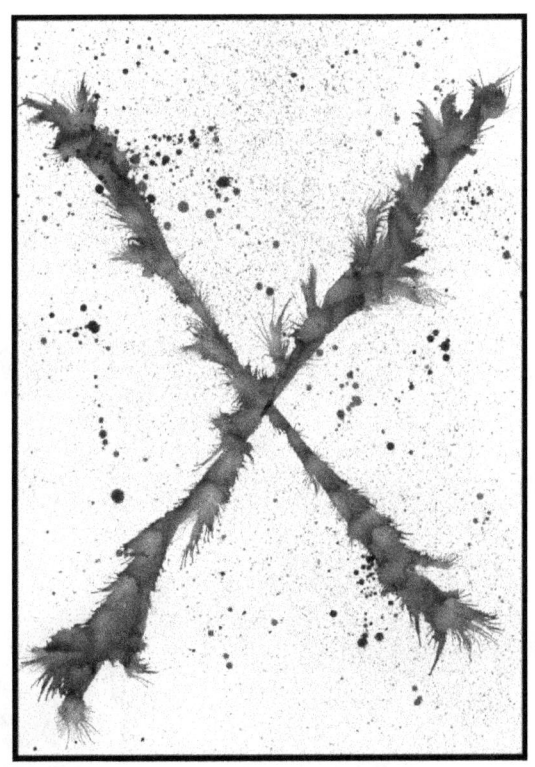

{A Soft Light}

Art is a soft light
in the dim of night.
Poetry is the boundless echo
of a soul's respite.

{Apocalypsis}

Metamorphosis
betwixt the old and the new.
Ashes bow to grace.

{Days of the Week}

Yesterday is a dream
we struggle to maintain.
Tomorrow is a memory
we have yet to obtain.
Today is a prisoner
we must strive to unchain.

{Beauty}

I choose to seek
the beauty in all things,
even those that may
trespass upon my heart
or relieve me of my trust.
I choose to do so
not because I seek
that which I lack,
but because not doing so
could strip me of the goodness
I may already possess
but have yet to discover.

{Dragon Tail}

Once again,
the earth shall assimilate you into herself.
You shall be broken down
and consumed -
overwhelmed by her appetite
as she restores the natural order
of her vast ecosystems.

Forgotten to time,
you shall return from whence you came -
into the dirt and sludge
of her belly.
Pure reincarnation,
recycled as fodder
for the yet living.

If you have lived well,
perhaps she will allow you to grow
into a mighty sequoia
and begin again.

{ Fire in the Sky }

We are all but specs of dust
exploding in the twilight
of someone else's night sky.

We are all but sweeping stars
arousing hopeful wishes
until we fade out and die.

None with breath are eternal,
mere residue left behind.
Take heed, for silence draws nigh.

{ I am }

I am every scattered light,
like a voice among the trees,
moving gentle with the breeze.

I am a shadow's echo,
like the face upon the moon
or a dream that fades too soon.

I am the last gasp you take
and your first eternal breath -
a shepherd beyond your death.

I am the key
to all that locks.
I am enigma -
the paradox.

You are that you are
for I am that I am.

{Knots}

somewhere between
love and hate
they reside

between the light
and the dark
they prefer to hover

on a tightrope
of right and wrong
they hide
behind a perceived balance
of obscurity and truth

they are the lawmakers
and land takers
the peacetalkers
and warmongers

the self-righteous
and the blameless
the hand shakers
and back stabbers
they are the loud speakers
and the no-doers

they conceal
their forked tongues
behind thin lips
fat lies
and alternative facts

they are the silent usurpers
and forgers of unnatural destinies
they are the creators of burden

and the erasers of lives
they are the antidote
to global unity
they are a plague
for which there is no cure

they are the paradoxical
the oxymoronical
the contradictions of words
versus results

between justice
and blind eyes
between moral betrayal
and "for the people"
they linger
hands waving
yet tied with
self
inflicted
knots

{Hollow}

Fill my coffers with riches
so I can feel just as hollow
as them.

{ Notes From the Past }

Look back,
look back
before you
leave me behind.

Look back,
look back
and you will
see me unwind.

Like a film of all
your missteps,
on a loop
within your mind.

Look back,
look back
one last time,
then leave me behind.

{ Pizza }

Ours is not to question.
Ours is only to accept
that nothing heals better

than a fresh, hot pizza.

{Shades}

There is poetry in darkness,
as well as the light.

{Renewed}

I vow to look
upon the world
with renewed eyes
each day that I am
privileged to do so.

{ Revelation }

Strip, peel, chip away.
Undress, remove, untie.
Slide off layer after layer,
exposing the truth
in my humility.

Collapse my shroud to the floor
and reveal me.

{Snake Skin}

I shed myself
like outgrown snake skin
leaving a hollow statue
in the wake of my footsteps.
A monument to the memory
of all the triumphs
and all the mistakes
that I must leave behind.
This constricting corset
of skewed self-identity
shall be purged
to make room for new growth.

{ Stormless }

Foolish is he who mistakes
my calm demeanor as meek.
Dragons dwell within me;
they rest in the quiet shadows
of my silence.

Tread lightly -
Who knows what slumbers
in the hollows of the stormless.

{ The White Dragon }

There is a dragon
gleaming white atop the hill.
His fiery call echoes
as smoke lingers still.

His claws dig into earth,
an example of malcontent.
Razors carving trenches
'til even the ground shall repent.

The bringer of flame has stirred
with a rumbling, smoldering quake.
The White Dragon cometh
with fire in his blistering wake.

{ To Love is to Learn }

Love knows not
of the boundaries of man.

Love does not
care for a well laid plan.

It can destroy and rebuild,
then ruin once more,

but lasts through infinitum
and will always restore.

{Vast}

The peaks of Carpathia.
The seas of Gallilee.
Our lunar landscape.
The depths of Europa.
The completeness of creation.
The vastness of our cosmos.
And the infinity of love.

{When the Heart Breaks}

When the sky breaks
it unleashes anger
like cracks upon glass
and echoes of light
like bombs in wartime.

When the clouds break
they unleash sadness
like tears from
forlorn eyes
or crashing waves
from restless seas.

When the heart breaks
it releases the full force
of a thousand lifetimes;
a thousand shattered souls
and forgotten dreams,
and a thousand
severed threads
that stitch the spirit within.

When the heart breaks
the sky cracks
and the clouds mourn

Savage Owl Press

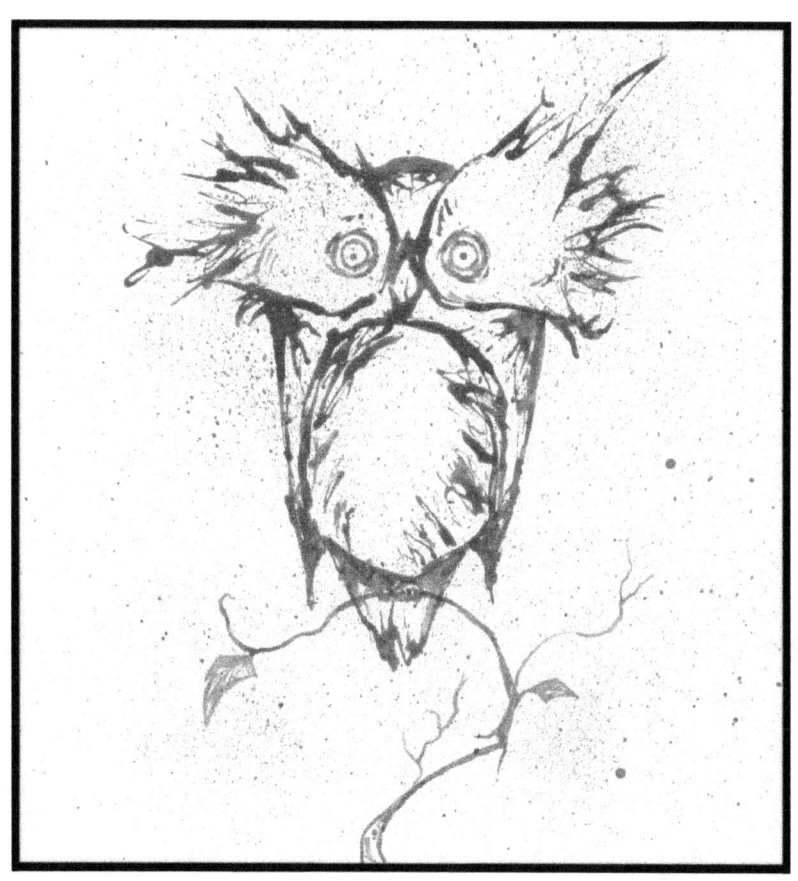

Thanks for reading *All These Broken Bones* by Kindred! Don't forget to leave an honest review – it means a lot to the author.

Also by Kindred:
Scattered Ink
Sun and Sky

All These Broken Bones by Kindred Cover by Kindred
Published by Savage Owl Press Dallas, TX

© 2019 Kindred
All rights reserved. No portion of this book may be reproduced in any form without permission from the publisher, except as permitted by U.S. copyright law. For permissions contact: permissions@savageowlpress.com

SavageOwlPress.com
@kindred.creates on instagram

ISBN-13: 978-1-7320549-4-3

www.ingramcontent.com/pod-product-compliance
Lightning Source LLC
Chambersburg PA
CBHW061326040426
42444CB00011B/2790